Robotics

FROM LEONARDO DA VINCI TO ISAAC ASIMOV

Jessie Alkire

Checkerboard
Library

An Imprint of Abdo Publishing
abdopublishing.com

ABDOPUBLISHING.COM

Published by Abdo Publishing, a division of ABDO, PO Box 398166, Minneapolis, Minnesota 55439.

Printed in the United States of America, North Mankato, Minnesota
052018
092018

Design and production: Mighty Media, Inc.
Editor: Liz Salzmann
Cover Photographs: Getty Images (right), Wikimedia Commons (left), Wikimedia Commons/with permission of Richard Greenhill and Hugo Elias (middle)
Interior Photographs: Alamy, p. 11; Anthony Quintano/Flickr, p. 27; AP Images, p. 23; Getty Images, pp. 15, 19; iStockphoto, pp. 4–5; Library of Congress, pp. 13, 28 (bottom); Mighty Media, Inc., p. 24; NASA/Wikimedia Commons, p. 17; Shutterstock, pp. 7, 21, 25, 29 (top, bottom); Wikimedia Commons, pp. 9, 28 (top)

Library of Congress Control Number: 2017961644

Publisher's Cataloging-in-Publication Data
Name: Alkire, Jessie, author.
Title: Robotics: From Leonardo da Vinci to Isaac Asimov / by Jessie Alkire.
Other titles: From Leonardo da Vinci to Isaac Asimov
Description: Minneapolis, Minnesota : Abdo Publishing, 2019. | Series: STEM stories | Includes online resources and index.
Identifiers: ISBN 9781532115486 (lib.bdg.) | ISBN 9781532156205 (ebook)
Subjects: LCSH: Robotics--Juvenile literature. | Robot industry--United States--Juvenile literature. | Inventors--Biography--Juvenile literature.
Classification: DDC 629.892--dc23

Contents

All About Robotics

Have you ever seen a robot in a movie? Was it helpful to humans? Or did it harm humans? Robots are a popular topic in science fiction. In fiction, robots are often seen as a symbol of a future where humans are ruled by machines. But many robots are used today to help humans.

Robotics is the creation and use of machines to do jobs or tasks. The first robots relied on moving mechanical parts. They could perform simple actions, such as move on their own. But the invention of the computer completely changed the future of robotics. Robots could be programmed to perform specific tasks.

Robotics is a popular subject for kids and adults alike. Many schools even offer robotics classes or clubs!

Today, robots are used in industries around the world. Robots are best at simple and **repetitive** tasks. They are also helpful in situations that would be too dangerous for humans, such as **defusing** bombs. Some robots even have human-like senses, such as sight, hearing, and touch.

All of these advances were accomplished by engineers and inventors throughout history. Today's **innovators** continue to come up with new ideas. Who knows what robots will be able to do in the future!

CHAPTER 1

Ancient Automatons

The first robots were very different from the robots of today. In fact, they weren't even called robots. These first robotic devices were known as automatons.

The first accounts of automatons date back to more than 2,000 years ago. People in ancient Greece and China were said to have created automatons for telling time and performing other simple tasks.

Many of these automatons were powered by water or steam. One of these was a steam-powered flying bird. It was designed by Greek mathematician Archytas.

Automatons continued to be developed in **medieval** times. Churches and other religious institutions often used automatons in worship. These automatons were human-like figures that could move around. Most people didn't understand that they moved mechanically. People believed a god or magical force was making them move.

Up until the 1400s, automatons remained simple mechanical devices. Many were **figurines** used to impress and entertain others. Then, Italian artist and inventor Leonardo da Vinci designed a new type of automaton.

An early automaton is the Astronomical Clock in Prague, Czech Republic. Each hour, sculptures of people and other figures move around as the clock chimes.

CHAPTER 2

The First Humanoid Robot

Da Vinci is best known for being a painter, but he was also an inventor and engineer. Some of his inventions were automatons. He wrote a lot about his work on these devices. Some of his ideas included a self-moving cart and a robotic lion!

One of da Vinci's most impressive automatons was a robotic knight. Da Vinci drew many extensive designs for his knight in the late 1400s. Some earlier automatons looked like people. However, none were as similar to the human body as da Vinci's knight. That's why it is considered the first humanoid robot.

Da Vinci's knight had cables to move different parts. The robot could sit up, lift its helmet's visor, turn its head, open and close its jaw, and more. Researchers aren't sure whether da Vinci actually built the knight. But in 2002, robotics expert Mark Rosheim built a model based on da Vinci's sketches. The robot worked exactly as da Vinci had designed it!

Leonardo da Vinci

BORN: April 15, 1452, Anchiano, Italy

DIED: May 2, 1519, Cloux, France (now Clos-Lucé, France)

FACT: Da Vinci was an Italian painter, sculptor, and inventor.

FACT: Da Vinci had 17 younger half-brothers and half-sisters.

FACT: In his teens, da Vinci received training in art from artist Andrea del Verrocchio.

ACHIEVEMENTS

- Da Vinci is most famous for his paintings, especially *Mona Lisa* and *The Last Supper*.
- Da Vinci was self-taught in science. He had notebooks full of inventions and scientific observations. He created designs for bicycles, helicopters, and submarines long before others had similar ideas.

STEM Star

CHAPTER 3

From Automatons to Robots

Inventors and engineers continued to design and build new automatons. One of these inventors was Jacques de Vaucanson. He built several automatons in the 1700s. These included a human figure that played the flute! Automatons by other inventors included moving animal figures, playing children, and more. Inventors would travel with their automatons to show them off to royalty and other wealthy people.

The popularity of automatons led scientists and writers to wonder about the effects they could have on people. English writer Mary Shelley published *Frankenstein* in 1818. The book discussed an artificial man that was brought to life and became violent toward its creator. *Frankenstein* is often considered one of the first texts to discuss artificial intelligence (AI).

In 1920, Czech writer Karel Capek wrote a play called *Rossum's Universal Robots*. In the play, human-like machines called robots took over the world and killed nearly every human. Capek was the first person to use the term *robot*. Capek later said

Jacques de Vaucanson (*standing*) created his flute player in 1737. It was the size of an adult human and could play 12 songs.

his brother, Josef, came up with the word. It comes from the Czech word *robota*. This means "forced labor." Soon after Capek's play came out, *robot* became the word commonly used for automatons.

CHAPTER 4

Robot Laws

In the 1900s, electrical power became easier to create and use. This helped engineers design robots powered by electricity. In 1942, American writer and scientist Isaac Asimov coined the term *robotics* for this new type of **technology**.

Asimov first used the term in a short story called "Runaround." The story takes place in a future in which robots are common. Asimov continued to explore robotics in other short stories. His stories were very popular. They also were many people's first introduction to robots and their possibilities.

"Runaround" also includes Asimov's Three Laws of Robotics. The first law is that robots can't harm humans. The second law is that robots must obey humans unless doing so would break the first law. The third law is that a robot must protect itself, unless doing so would break the first or second laws.

The Three Laws have been used mostly by science fiction authors. But the laws help robotics experts keep robot **ethics** in mind. This can help keep both robots and humans safe.

Isaac Asimov

BORN: January 2, 1920, Petrovichi, Russia

DIED: April 6, 1992, New York City, New York

FACT: Asimov was an American writer and chemist.

FACT: After college, Asimov taught **biochemistry** at the Boston University School of Medicine.

FACT: Asimov published nearly 500 books.

STEM Star

ACHIEVEMENTS

- Asimov earned a master's degree and PhD in chemistry from Columbia University in New York City.
- Asimov is best known for his science fiction books and short stories. In 1950, nine of Asimov's short stories were combined into the book *I, Robot*. In 2004, the book was made into a movie of the same name featuring actor Will Smith.
- Asimov coined the term *robotics*.
- Asimov wrote the Three Laws of Robotics.

CHAPTER 5

The Birth of the Modern Robot

Asimov and other science fiction writers explored how robots might look and behave. But it was **technology** that brought these ideas to life. The first electronic robot amazed **audiences** at the 1939 New York World's Fair.

This robot was called Elektro. It was invented by the Westinghouse Electric Company. An operator used electronic controls to make Elektro walk, move its arms, and speak recorded statements.

This technology was so new that Elektro's creators worried that people would think there was a person inside Elektro. So, they included a hole in Elektro's body so people could see inside it. This proved all of its actions were done electronically.

The next advancement in robotics came in the 1940s. British robotics expert William Grey Walter invented two robots named Elmer and Elsie in 1948 and 1949. Elmer and Elsie had **dome**-shaped covers and moved slowly, so they were often called robot tortoises.

William Grey Walter created Elmer and Elsie to better understand the human brain. He wanted to learn how the brain processes information to make choices about behavior.

Unlike Elektro, Elmer and Elsie didn't need an operator to control all of their actions. These robots had light and touch **sensors** that helped them find their way. They even knew to travel to a charging station when their batteries ran low.

The first programmable industrial robot was invented by American engineer George Devol in 1954. It was a robotic arm called Unimate. Devol and fellow American engineer Joseph Engelberger formed the company Unimation Inc. to manufacture Unimates. Each one weighed 4,000 pounds (1,814 kg)!

In 1961, automobile manufacturer General Motors started using a Unimate on its assembly line. The Unimate was mostly used for **welding** and other metalworking tasks. These tasks were difficult and dangerous for humans to perform. Metalwork usually requires heating metal to extremely high temperatures. It was easy for a metalworker to get burned. Other automobile companies soon began employing Unimates too. Soon, Unimates were also used in Europe and Asia.

Devol and Engelberger's success with Unimate proved robotics could be a profitable business. Unimate also showed that robots could replace humans for certain tasks, particularly in manufacturing. New and improved robotic arms were soon developed to make manufacturing safer and more **efficient**.

Unimation later developed another robotic arm called the PUMA. In the 1990s, NASA used a PUMA at its Ames Research Center in Silicon Valley, California.

CHAPTER 6

New and Improved

The 1960s and 1970s were full of changes and improvements for robots. **Technology** was advancing quickly. Computers, batteries, and other robot parts were getting smaller and lighter. Robotic arms were a main area of development at this time. While Unimate was successful, scientists wanted to create lighter, more **versatile** robots.

One such robot was the Stanford Arm. This robot was invented in 1969 by American engineer Victor Scheinman at Stanford University. The Stanford Arm was fully controlled by a computer. It had **sensors** that allowed it to see and feel its surroundings. Like Unimate, the Stanford Arm was mostly used in automobile manufacturing.

Another robot was invented around the same time as the Stanford Arm. Shakey was developed from 1966 to 1972 by researchers from the Stanford Research Institute. Shakey was the first robot controlled by AI. It could move around, make plans, and arrange objects.

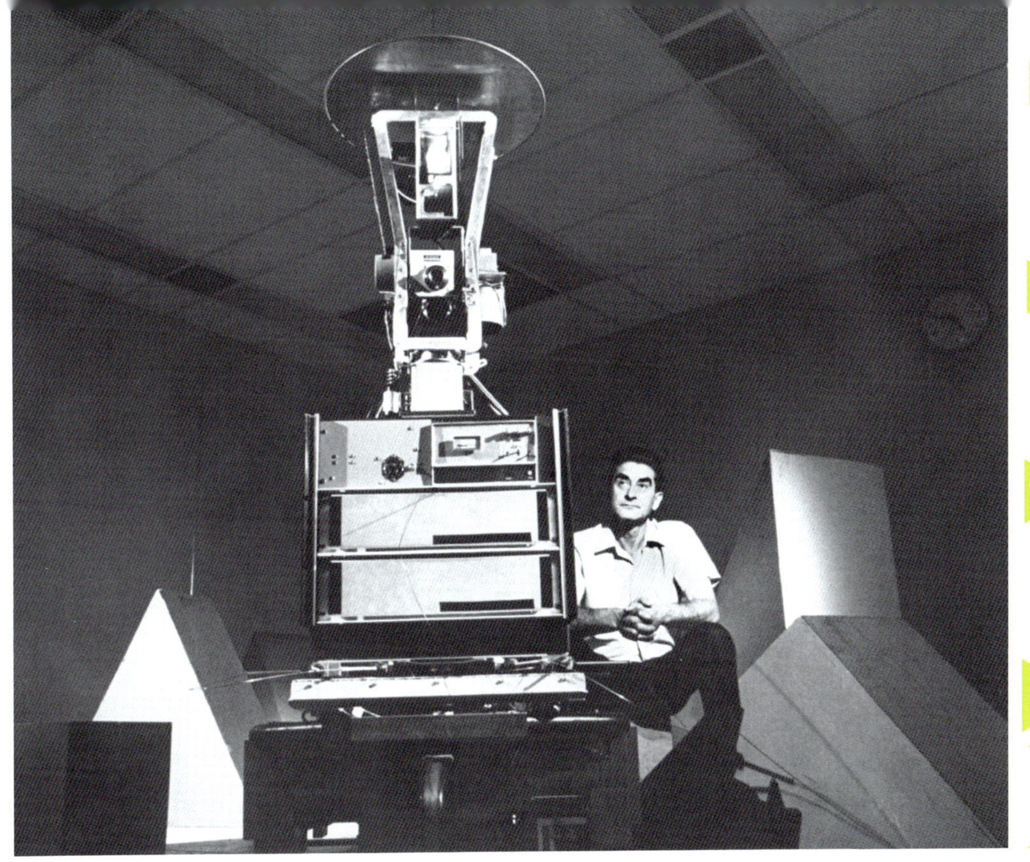

Computer scientist Charles Rosen was on the team that developed Shakey. Shakey got its name because it tended to shake as it moved.

A combination of parts and computer **software** helped Shakey understand its surrounding and move around. The robot had **sensors**, lasers, and a camera to provide data. Shakey was specially programmed to solve problems, such as getting past unexpected obstacles. It was also connected to a computer by radio links so the computer could send Shakey specific commands. *Life* magazine called Shakey "the first electronic person."

CHAPTER 7

Robots for People

Throughout the 1970s, public interest in robots increased. This was due to news coverage of developments in robotics, such as Shakey. During this time, science fiction books and movies continued to be popular.

One of the most successful movies to feature robot characters was *Star Wars: A New Hope*. It was released in 1977. Two of the characters were robots, C-3PO and R2-D2. Since then, eight additional *Star Wars* movies have been made, all featuring these and other robots.

Toy robots were also popular during this time. Toy companies started releasing more advanced toy robots. One such robot was the Omnibot 2000. This remote-controlled robot was released in 1985. It could move, talk, and carry objects. A tape recorder in its chest could receive commands or words to be played back.

As **technology** advanced, robot developers could make robots that looked and acted more like people. In 2000, Japanese company Honda developed a human-like robot called ASIMO.

R2-D2 (*right*) entered the Robot Hall of Fame in 2003. C-3PO (*left*) was added the following year.

It was designed to be a robot companion. The child-sized robot could walk, climb, and avoid obstacles. It could also "see" through a camera and recognize people, gestures, and movement.

CHAPTER 8

Today's Technology

Many recent advancements in robotics have been shown to help humans. One area in which this is happening is healthcare and medicine. In 2000, the US Food and Drug Administration approved the da Vinci Surgical System. This is a robot with four arms. Surgeons control the arms with foot pedals and levers. This system helps surgeons be more precise. It also inspired many other surgical robot inventions.

A recent development in robotics is AI. AI is the ability of a machine to display human-like qualities, such as emotions, awareness, and independent thinking. The latest robots also look more like real humans than ever before.

These robots are often called *ultra-realistic*. They wear clothes and have human-like skin and hair. Ultra-realistic robots can even have personalities and human-like facial expressions. One ultra-realistic robot is Sophia. Sophia was unveiled by Chinese company Hanson Robotics in 2015. Sophia has been on several television shows, including *60 Minutes* and *The Tonight Show*.

Robots like Sophia are known as social robots. They can express emotions, recognize people, and hold conversations. This helps people form relationships with the robots. Researchers think this type of robot can provide social interaction for sick people, children, and the elderly.

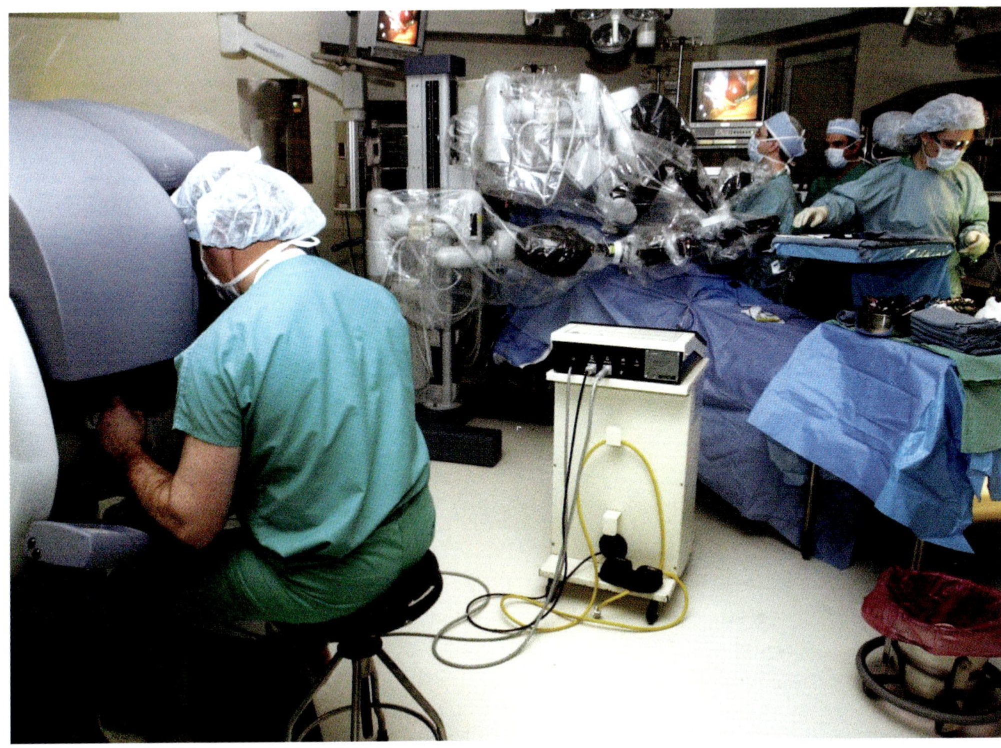

A surgeon operates the da Vinci Surgical System from a computer station several feet away from the patient. Monitors show other members of the surgical team what the robot is doing.

Robots:

PAST AND PRESENT

Automatons, such as da Vinci's knight, had mechanical parts that allowed them to move. These parts included gears, cables, and pulleys. Modern humanoid robots, such as Sophia, use cameras, **sensors**, and computer **technology** to move and speak.

DA VINCI'S KNIGHT

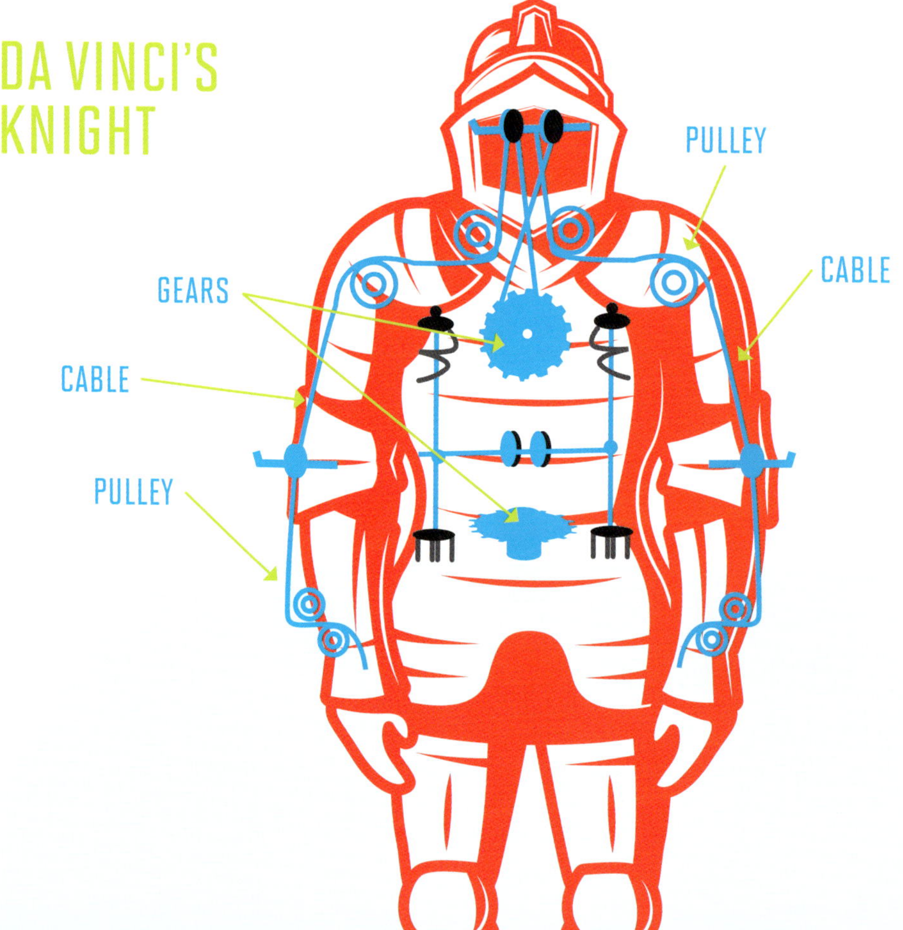

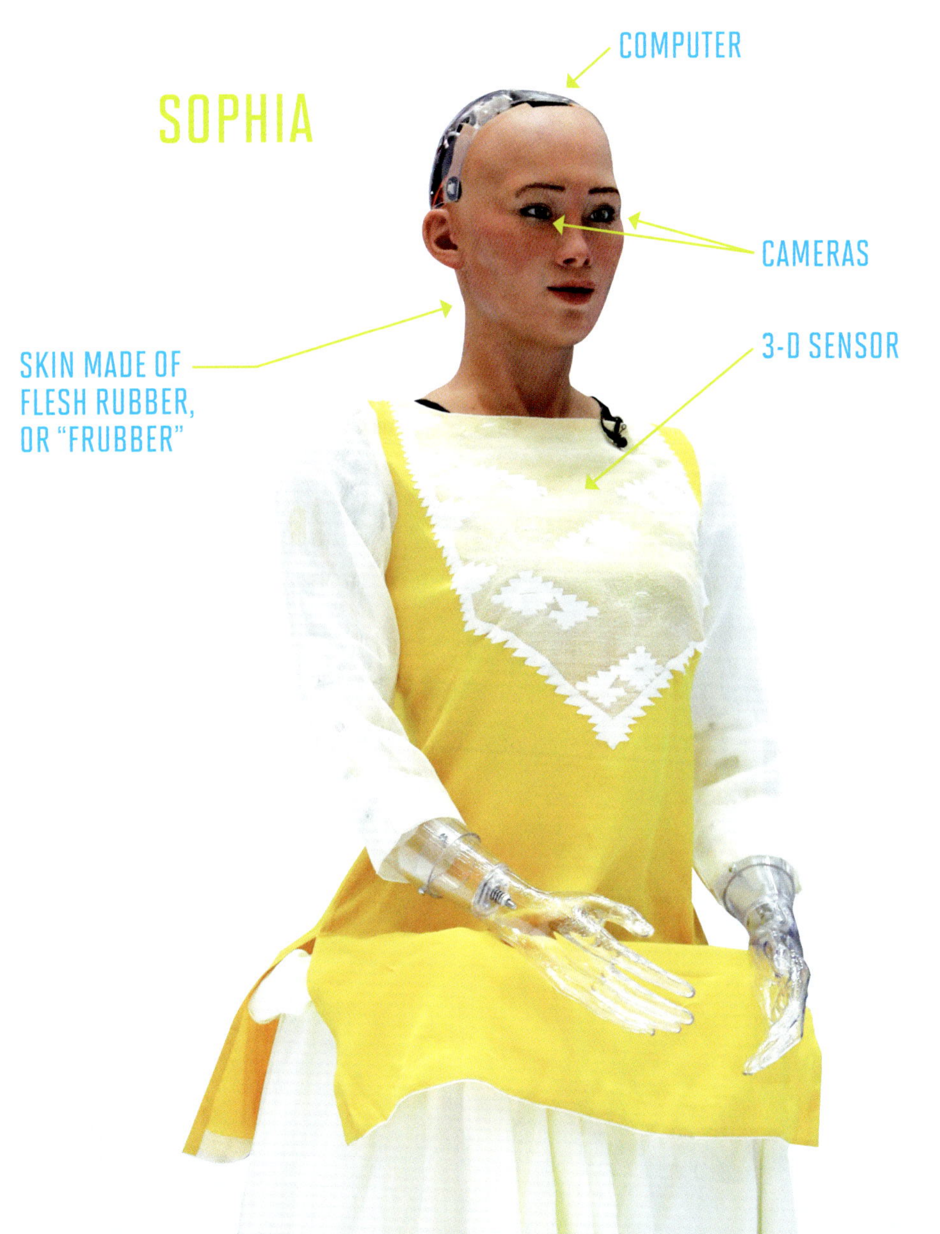
SOPHIA
COMPUTER
CAMERAS
3-D SENSOR
SKIN MADE OF
FLESH RUBBER,
OR "FRUBBER"

CHAPTER 9

The Future of Robotics

It's possible that humans and robots will develop a close relationship in the future. This is especially likely in business. Businesses want to have the cheapest and most **efficient** workers possible. Intelligent robots could fill these positions.

Many researchers want ultra-realistic robots to understand the human experience. These researchers believe this will allow humans and robots to work together to solve scientific questions. However, some people worry robots will become too intelligent. They fear robots will get out of control and harm humans.

Experts such as American **entrepreneur** Elon Musk agree that AI could be dangerous. Musk worries that eventually robots will be able to do too many jobs better than humans. This could cause people to lose their jobs. Musk also believes that AI development should be carefully **monitored** and regulated to keep people safe.

But others don't think people should be afraid of AI. Mark Zuckerberg, who founded **social media** site Facebook, believes AI will be very beneficial to people. He said, "In the next five to ten

Zuckerberg thinks one of the main benefits of AI is safety. He believes technologies such as self-driving cars and robot doctors could make the world safer for humans.

years, AI is going to deliver so many improvements in the quality of our lives."

In spite of disagreements about AI, engineers continue to develop more advanced robots. Who knows what **innovations** will come next? A robotic future might not be far away!

Timeline

late 1400s Leonardo da Vinci designs a humanoid robot knight.

1920 Karel Capek coins the term *robot* in his play *Rossum's Universal Robots*.

1939 The robot Elektro is introduced at the New York World's Fair.

1942 Isaac Asimov coins the term *robotics* and writes the Three Laws of Robotics in his story "Runaround."

1954 George Devol invents the robotic arm Unimate.

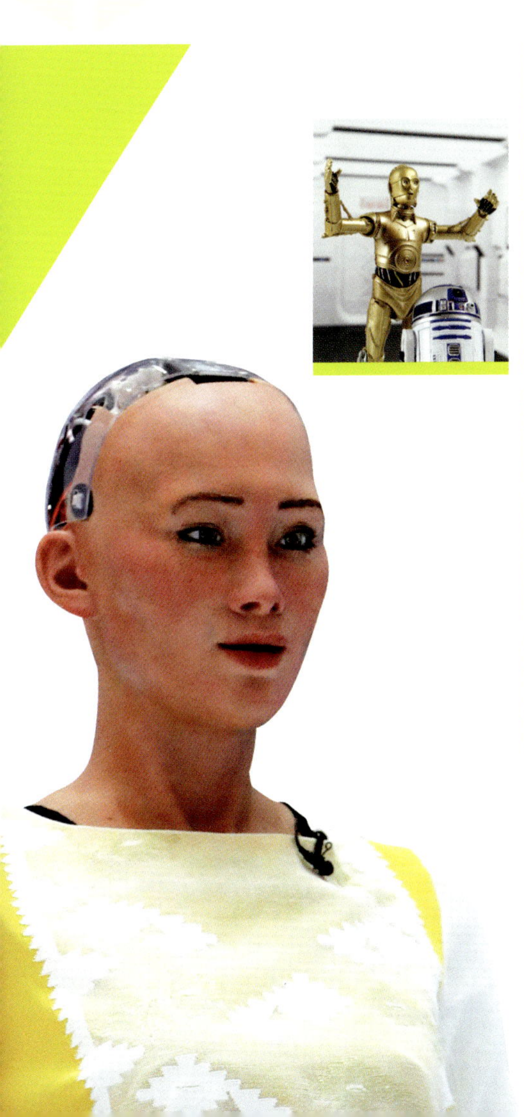

1966–1972 Researchers at the Stanford Research Institute develop the robot Shakey.

1977 The movie *Star Wars: A New Hope* introduces robots C-3PO and R2-D2.

1985 Toy robot Omnibot 2000 is released.

2000 The FDA approves the da Vinci Surgical System.

2015 Ultra-realistic social robot Sophia is unveiled.

Glossary

audience—a group of people watching a performance.

biochemistry—the chemistry of living things.

defuse—to make a bomb unable to explode.

dome—a rounded top.

efficient—wasting little time or energy.

entrepreneur—one who organizes, manages, and accepts the risks of a business or an enterprise.

ethics—the rules of moral conduct followed by a person or group.

figurine—a small statue.

innovator—a person who comes up with a new idea, method, or device. Their creation is called an innovation.

medieval (mee-DEE-vuhl)—of or belonging to the Middle Ages. The Middle Ages was a period in European history from about 500 CE to 1500 CE.

monitor—to watch, keep track of, or oversee.

repetitive—having parts or actions that are repeated many times.

sensor—an instrument that can detect, measure, and transmit information to a controlling device.

social media—forms of electronic communication that allow people to create online communities to share information, ideas, and messages. Facebook, Instagram, and Snapchat are examples of social media.

software—the written programs used to operate a computer.

technology (tehk-NAH-luh-jee)—machinery and equipment developed for practical purposes using scientific principles and engineering.

versatile—having many uses.

weld—to join metal parts using heat.

Online Resources

To learn more about robotics, visit **abdobooklinks.com**. These links are routinely monitored and updated to provide the most current information available.

Index